HAY BALERS

By E.T. Weingarten

Gareth Stevens
PUBLISHING

Please visit our website, www.garethstevens.com. For a free color catalog of all our high-quality books, call toll free 1-800-542-2595 or fax 1-877-542-2596.

Library of Congress Cataloging-in-Publication Data

Names: Weingarten, E. T., author.
Title: Hay balers / E. T. Weingarten.
Other titles: Fantastic farm machines.
Description: New York : Gareth Stevens Publishing, [2016] | Series: Fantastic farm machines | Includes index.
Identifiers: LCCN 2016001338 | ISBN 9781482445923 (pbk.) | ISBN 9781482445848 (library bound) | ISBN 9781482445725 (6 pack)
Subjects: LCSH: Harvesting machinery–Juvenile literature. | Haying equipment–Juvenile literature. | Baling–Equipment and supplies–Juvenile literature.
Classification: LCC S695 .W45 2016 | DDC 631.3–dc23
LC record available at http://lccn.loc.gov/2016001338

Published in 2017 by
Gareth Stevens Publishing
111 East 14th Street, Suite 349
New York, NY 10003

Designer: Sarah Liddell
Editor: Therese Shea

Photo credits: Cover, p. 1 Echo/Cultura/Getty Images; spread background texture used throughout LongQuattro/Shutterstock.com; p. 5 Marius C/Shutterstock.com; p. 7 ericlefrancais/Shutterstock.com; p. 9 jeka84/Shutterstock.com; pp. 11 (mower), 17 TFoxFoto/Shutterstock.com; p. 11 (hay rake) Flickr upload bot/Wikimedia Commons; p. 13 Daplaza/Wikimedia Commons; p. 15 CHere/Shutterstock.com; p. 19 Nancy Nehring/Moment Mobile/Getty Images; p. 21 Steve Heap/Shutterstock.com.

Printed in the United States of America

CPSIA compliance information: Batch #CS16GS: For further information contact Gareth Stevens, New York, New York at 1-800-542-2595.

CONTENTS

Boldface words appear in the glossary.

Hey, It's Hay!

Have you ever seen a field full of tightly packed piles of hay? These are called bales. Did you ever wonder how farmers make them? They use farm machines called hay balers. The hay is for animals!

Hay is the food that cattle, horses, and other farm animals eat. They need a lot of this food in winter when the plants they eat aren't growing in the fields. Hay has **nutrients** the animals need.

Hay is made from grasses or **legumes**. It can also be a cereal. That's a plant that produces **grain**, such as wheat or oats. To become hay, crops are cut when they're flowering. They're often cured, or dried, in the sun.

wheat

Cutting the Crop

It takes a lot of work to cut and gather hay by hand. Luckily, farmers have machines to help them. They use mowers to cut the crop. They use hay rakes to turn over the cut hay so it dries fully.

mower

hay rake

11

Hay that isn't dried can spoil, or rot. Curing also makes it taste better to the animals! The hay rake puts the hay into a long row called a windrow. When the hay is ready, the farmer uses the hay baler.

13

How It Works

A tractor pulls the hay baler. A spool of teeth called a pickup gathers the hay in the windrow. The hay is fed into a **chamber** where a **plunger** packs and cuts the hay into a certain shape.

pickup

After the hay baler collects an amount of hay, a special tool ties the bale with string or wire. It only takes a few seconds! Then, the bale is pushed through a **chute** onto the ground.

17

Small square bales of hay may weigh up to 70 pounds (32 kg) each. A large round hay bale can weigh 2,000 pounds (907 kg)! More machines may help gather the bales to keep the hay from being spoiled by rain.

Ready When Needed

Finished hay bales are stored in a dry place, such as a barn or **silo**. The hay is fed to animals when it's needed. Both farmers and their animals need the fantastic farm machines called hay balers!

GLOSSARY

chamber: a small space inside something

chute: a pipe something can slide down

grain: the seeds of plants (such as wheat, corn, and rice) that are used for food

legume: a type of plant such as a pea or a bean plant with seeds that grow in long cases

nutrient: something a living thing needs to grow and stay alive

plunger: a part that moves up and down in order to push something

silo: a tall, narrow building that's used to store food for farm animals

FOR MORE INFORMATION

BOOKS

Alexander, Heather. *All Around the Farm*. New York, NY: Parachute Press/DK Publishing, 2007.

Coppendale, Jean. *Tractors and Farm Vehicles*. Richmond Hill, Ontario, Canada: Firefly Books, 2010.

Rosen, Michael J. *Our Farm: Four Seasons with Five Kids on One Family's Farm*. Plain City, OH: Darby Creek Publishing, 2008.

WEBSITES

Straw vs. Hay
www.usaforage.org/products/straw-vs-hay/
Learn the difference between these two farm products.

Tools of the Trade: Choosing a Hay Baler
www.hobbyfarms.com/farm-equipment-and-tools/ choosing-a-hay-baler-22047.aspx
Read more about farming hay, past and present.

INDEX